THE FRESCOES BY ANGELICO AT SAN MARCO

The frescoes by Angelico at San Marco

Magnolia Scudieri

GIUNTI FIRENZE MVSEI

www.giunti.it

ISBN 88-09-03749-9

© 2004 Ministero per i Beni e le Attività Culturali –
Soprintendenza Speciale per il Polo Museale Fiorentino
First edition: July 2004

FIRENZE MVSEI is a registered trademark
created by Sergio Bianco

Photographic credits:
Archivio Fotografico SBAS, Archivio Giunti/Stefano Giraldi,
Archivio Giunti/Domingie-Rabatti, Nicolò Orsi Battaglini,
Antonio Quattrone, Rabatti & Domingie Photography – Florence

Editorial production of
Giunti Editore S.p.A., Florence-Milan

Editorial manager: Claudio Pescio
Editor: Augusta Tosone
Project design and layout: Carlo Savona
Floor plans: Stefano Benini
Translation: Joan M. Reifsnyder

Reprints	Year
5 4 3 2 1 0	2007 2006 2005 2004

Printed by Giunti Industrie Grafiche S.p.A. - Prato

INDEX

Finally! This is the type of guidebook I would like to see in all our museums. It is well illustrated and printed, the price is reasonable, and it fully treats a single topic, one that is dominant and central to the Museum.

Visitors come to San Marco for Fra Angelico, and what especially interests them are Angelico's frescoes. Ascending to the upper floor, and finding the *Annunciation* on the landing, it seems as if you have just stepped into Paradise. The images living in the silence of the cells are perfect illustrations of 'visible prayer': the *Crucifixion* in the Chapter Room, a masterpiece of tender, melancholic humanity is at the same time the apex of theological thought. With limpid clarity, this book by Magnolia Scudieri director of the Museum, accompanies our visit to the frescoes. One immediately sees that behind each entry there is detailed knowledge of the studies done on Angelico's cycle of frescoes in San Marco. But academic knowledge and scholarship are only the skeleton; the text must be exact, well developed, precise in every historical or descriptive detail. The author makes sure that each work of art is understood by the viewer-reader: understood in terms of the iconographic subject, the symbolic meaning, the attribution, the important stylistic traits. Read the entry for the *Annunciation*, frescoed in Cell 3. You will agree with me that the description could not be more 'scientific', more professional, clearer, more understandable and didactically exemplary than in this entry. When writing about Angelico, it is all too easy (and dangerous) to become sidetracked into generic mysticism and poor literature.

Guido di Piero upon entering the Dominican order took the name Giovanni, but he is known throughout the world by his heavenly alias, Angelico. He was a philosopher and theologian, a man of science and learning. He believed that reason allows us to approach the edge of mystery, and that painting was an intellectual tool capable of rendering comprehensible, and above all enticing, the highest values in Christian spiritualism. I am confident you will appreciate the exemplary didactic work done on Angelico by Magnolia Scudieri.

The Superintendent
for Polo Museale Fiorentino
Antonio Paolucci

Mocking of Christ, with the Virgin
and Saint Dominic *(Cell 7),*
detail of Saint Dominic.

Annunciation,
detail of a capital;
North Corridor-
Corridor of the Lay Brothers.

THE MUSEUM OF SAN MARCO is renowned not only for its works by Fra Angelico, but for the numerous examples of Florentine art and for the pervasive history of the Dominican Order. The presence of the fresco cycle by the great friar-artist makes it a sanctuary for Angelico's art, and transforms the Convent into one of the most important sites for early Renaissance painting. The large number of frescoes, their specific destination and function, represent a unique moment for all painting, not just Florentine, at the beginning of the *Quattrocento.*

The full understanding and appreciation of artworks in today's museum may prove difficult at times due to the fact they are removed from their historical and physical context.

This is not the case with the frescoes by Fra Angelico in San Marco. They have remained in their original location in the Dominican convent, built by Michelozzo and financed by Cosimo de' Medici, the Elder. Most of the convent has remained unaltered; thus the frescoes can still be viewed in relation to the architectural structure and convent life of the period.

During the sixteenth and seventeenth centuries, as a result of structural renovations, a *Crucifixion* by Angelico was demolished along with the Refectory wall, and a few frescoes in the cells in the north dormitory on the upper floor were lost, consequence of opening a window onto the Cloister.

During the 1600s other modifications saw the frescoed lunettes by Angelico in the Cloister made part of a narrative cycle dedicated to Saint Antonino.

Nonetheless, the meaning and significance in the art by the friar-artist of San Marco has remained intact and perfectly appreciable.

The knowledge and understanding of the artist became even more complete around 1925, when a major portion of his works on wood panel, executed for Florence-area churches and convents, entered the Gallerie Fiorentine as a result of suppression of religious orders in the eighteenth-nineteenth centuries. Being able to view the panel paintings and frescoes next to each other helps in understanding the diversity of Angelico's artist expression in relation to the destination of the work and its patron.

Angelico did not dwell on narrative or decorative elements in the frescoes in San Marco, as was typical for the paintings displayed to the public in the churches, meant to help understand the Holy Scriptures. The friars living in the convent were already very familiar with them. Their mission was to preach, to further knowledge about the mysteries, best called to mind using symbolic images.

The originality of the cycle of frescoes is aimed and directed exclusively towards a select and learned public: the Dominican brothers. The images frescoed on the interior or exterior walls throughout the large monastic complex, needed to be functional to the cloistered life in the convent, a means of conveying didactic and contemplative messages through of continual reference models found in Christ, the Virgin Mary, Saint Dominic and the Order's first saints, Peter of Verona and Thomas Aquinas.

The figurative language is appropriate to this goal; it is clear, simple, intensely emotional, rationally laid out and spiritually expressive.

Only a little more than ten years after Masaccio painted his frescoes in the Brancacci Chapel, Angelico answered the call to artistic revolution on a different, even though parallel, path.

The Giottesque naturalistic tradition to which both these artists belong, completely overturned in Masaccio by a new expressive force separating the form, the drawing, the volume, is translated in Angelico into rational analysis of reality, of man and his relation to his surroundings, constantly illuminated and sublimated in dialogue with God.

In the San Marco frescoes there is an exceptional symbiosis between realism and surrealism, spirituality and naturalism, tradition and innovation, sanctity and humanity, aimed not at relating sacred history, but in expressing with the greatest simplicity and intensity, the love uniting the sons of Saint Dominic to Jesus Christ.

When looking at the frescoes in San Marco, it is important to always keep in mind the end-user and purpose, in order to understand the value contained in the new naturalistic and rational images in which the story or the individual is placed. The art here is not meant to broaden knowledge, but is an object for meditation, valuable in expressing and eliciting mystical emotion, the joy of prayer, the willingness to emulate.

Before setting off on the visit, it is useful to trace the historical events that preceded and accompanied the painting of these frescoes.

Annunciation,
detail of the Virgin Annunciate;
North Corridor-Corridor
of the Lay Brothers.

The new convent of San Marco

SINCE THE 1200s, the convent and church of San Marco had been occupied by the Silvestrine monks. However in 1436, Pope Eugene IV definitively assigned the complex to the Reformed Dominicans at San Domenico di Fiesole. For quite a while, they had hoped to obtain a site in the city in order to more effectively propagate the spirit of renewal in the Observance movement. The Observance was guided at the time by Antonino Pierozzi, 'son' of the convent in Fiesole, who was named Vicar General of the movement in 1432. Before Antonino was named Archbishop of Florence in 1446, and during the reconstruction period, he served as prior at San Marco.

The positive outcome of the Dominican bid for the convent was influenced by a series of favourable events. During this period, the papal court of Pope Eugene IV was present in Florence, member of which was the Observant Dominican theologian, John of Torquemada. The unconditional support of influential individuals such as Cosimo and Lorenzo de' Medici, who had already helped in supporting the Reformed Franciscans at Bosco ai Frati, must have helped the Dominicans' case. Cosimo was a rich and cultured banker, and after his return from exile in Padua, he was named Gonfalonier of Florence in 1435, the same period he donated the funds necessary to renovate the convent and church, both in a state of ruin. He also made funds available to sustain the basic needs of the community of friars, bound by the vow of poverty.

The renovation work for the complex was given to Michelozzo, an architect who was well favoured by Cosimo. However, work did not actually start until two years after the Dominicans had taken up residence, at the end of 1437, after they had won the appeal put forth by the Silvestrines.

The pre-existing buildings were incorporated into the new convent, and according to Giorgio Vasari, building continued until 1452. But, in the convent's *Cronaca* compiled by Fra Giuliano Lapaccini and the prior between 1444-1445 and 1448-1453, a much earlier conclusion date, 1443, is given. This was followed in 1444 by the completion of the Library, which was grafted onto the north wing after it had already been finished.

The sequence in which the work developed is not fully understood, and from the documents it seems to have been intermittent, slowed by the need to inter-

*Aerial view
of the San Marco complex
with the church and the convent.*

vene on the church, and exacerbated by the death of one of the benefactors, Lorenzo de' Medici, in 1440.

The construction began in 1437 with the east wing, and the first dormitory with twenty cells was constructed above the Refectory. Between 1438 and 1439, the only major work recorded in the *Cronaca* was done on the church. Other documents attest to the fact that in 1441 work was underway for the north wing, finished in 1442. There is no information about construction of the south dormitory, probably built at the same time as the north wing, or immediately afterward, and in any case within 1443. Most likely it was finished for Epiphany of that year when the church was consecrated by Pope Eugene IV, who spent the night in the cell reserved for Cosimo de' Medici, the last one on the north side towards the second cloister. Even though the *Cronaca* specifies that the convent was not yet fully completed, it seems logical that the areas dedicated to the main functions were ready, liveable and probably already frescoed. This hypothesis opens the discussion about the dating of the frescoes, a topic we will address further on.

The Dominicans wanted all the meaningful and important points of the convent to be enriched by fresco images having symbolic value, so the brothers would be continually called to the observance of the principles in the *Constitutiones*. Visual reminders of the close relationship with Jesus Christ, for whom devotion and continual dialogue were fundamental in the Rule of Saint Dominic, invited the brothers to follow his example. It is evident that the images were meant to visually illustrate the dictates of the *Constitutiones*, to educate the younger brothers in the way of prayer according to Saint Dominic, to constantly renew the invitation to humility and charity. In order to be completely effective, the images also had to be emotionally moving, to motivate reflection and to strengthen the desire to emulate the love shed on mankind by Jesus Christ though his ultimate sacrifice. It seems obvious that an illustrative program of these dimensions, closely inspired by the guidelines of the Observance, movement dear to Antonino Pierozzi, the prior in the convent between 1439 and 1444, could be given only to Fra Giovanni of Fiesole. In addition to being brother in the Order, promoter of the Observance, son of the convent at San Domenico from which the first nucleus of brothers left for San Marco, he was also one of the major artists at the time in Florence, referred to even by his fellow artists as, *pictor angelicus*.

Christ on the Cross
adored by Saint Dominic,
detail of Saint Dominc's hand;
Cloister of Sant'Antonino.

Angelico and San Marco

(Angelico' is the epithet given to the painter shortly after his death. He was baptised Guido and, his father's name being Piero, was known as Guido di Piero. He came from near Castello di Vicchio in the Mugello area north of Florence, and when he joined the Order at the San Domenico convent in about 1420, he took the name Giovanni. His birth date is unknown, but thought to be around 1400.

Even though relatively little is still known about his training and early activity, there are two certainties that emerge from the documents. We know that he was already painting in 1417, and, that he was always strongly tied to and remained part of the San Domenico community, repeatedly taking on the role of the convent's Vicar in 1431, 1432, 1436, and 1450, and where he executed some of his most beautiful paintings and frescoes.

It is quite probable that at the San Domenico convent he had a space to use as a workshop where he could comfortably carry out work as a panel painter, intensely active between 1420 and 1440.

This hypothesis in no way contrasts with the claustral rule if we remember the apostolic aim of his activity and the fact that the proceeds of his painting, as evidenced by various documents, went to help support the convent and community life.

His temporary presence at San Marco is documented at two community meetings: one in the new Sacristy in 1441, and the other in the new Chapter Room in 1442.

His participation was probably motivated by the work-in-progress on the frescoes, and by the fact that until 1445, the San Domenico and San Marco convents were under a single administration. In the late 1430s, at the height of his activity, he had commissions both in and out of Florence, as documented in a famous letter written in 1438 by the painter Domenico Veneziano.

In 1445, when the work on the new convent was completed and the number of novices had sizeably increased, it was proposed that the two convents separate. Angelico was in favour of the separation and was subsequently assigned to the convent at San Domenico. All this leads to the supposition that his commitment at San Marco was concluded by that point.

Presentation in the Temple
(Cell 10), detail
of the elderly priest Simeon
with the Infant Christ.

Dating the frescoes

THE MOST ACCREDITED HYPOTHESIS today dates the frescoes between 1438 and 1443, at the latest 1445. Some scholars (Hood, Bellosi) have recently reiterated their conviction that the frescoes in the north dormitory cells and the three on the corridor walls were painted around 1450. It is certainly true that the stylistic changes within the cycle point to different stages in the execution of the frescoes, painted at intervals of a few years from one another. It is also true that some of the stylistic discrepancies can be explained by the presence of collaborators, and even though completely faithful to the *maestro's* dictates, there are different characteristics and levels of quality. In the absence of solid documentation regarding either the dates or the collaborators, the scholarly debate is still open and lively.

The attempt to isolate Angelico's work from that of his collaborators and to identify them, has been repeatedly undertaken by scholars. Apart from identifying some interventions by Benozzo Gozzoli, this effort has not brought fully acceptable and unequivocal results. The positions on the subject are at two extremes: the scholars (Pope-Hennessy, Hood) who contend that collaborators did much of the work, and those (Boskovits) who exclude almost entirely any collaborative assistance.

The intermediate positions hold that Angelico carried out most of the work, with limited assistance by Benozzo Gozzoli (Bellosi), or with Gozzoli's more incisive collaboration (Padoa Rizzo, Bonsanti), evidenced in the *Adoration of the Magi* and the novices' cells,

as well as in some passages in the first corridor cells, and in many of the North Corridor cells.

This is a fairly complex problem because the *Cronaca* assigns the cycle solely to Fra Giovanni, referring to the homogeneity manifested by a single creative mind, notwithstanding a progressive transformation in the expressive mode due to the different locations of the frescoes and the ultimate destination of the space. It appears certain that Angelico conceived and drew all the frescoes, first on the *arriccio* plaster layer in red (the *sinopia*), and then in olive green pigment on the *intonaco* plaster, often visible through the overlying pictorial layer.

He also closely followed his collaborator's work, so as to obtain a final painting that was faithful to his concept and pictorial style. During this historical period in art, the painting profession usually required a collective work structure with well-defined tasks based on individual roles – apprentice, assistant or collaborator – and always under the direct supervision of the *maestro* or principal. Given the very high quality of the work, it is not easy to detect stylistic variations between the collaborators and Angelico, especially on work most likely made over the course of time.

The only exceptions to these doubts are the areas with obvious differences in quality or having different expressive purposes. Within any given fresco, these distinctions must be viewed by an attentive (not always easy) examination of the *giornate*, the individually painted sections that when combined together constitute the whole of each fresco.

In addition to firmly identifying the parts of the work executed by assistants, there is also the difficulty of identifying the artists in the group of traditionally known followers – Benozzo Gozzoli, Zanobi Strozzi, Domenico di Michelino – or other painters in Angelico's entourage. All three known followers were young painters between the ages of seventeen (Gozzoli) and twenty-five (Strozzi), and all were newly independent painters or still working in their role as 'disciples'. There are almost no works with which to make a comparison by these artists prior to 1438, the hypothetical date of the start of the frescoes in the First Corridor cells. On the other hand, given Angelico's strong conceptual and formal imprint on the cycle, conclusive identification of the individual artist (if such is the case) responsible for the execution is not absolutely necessary in order to read, understand and enjoy these frescoes.

Annunciation *(Cell 3),*
detail of the Virgin's mantle;
the underdrawing
by Angelico in olive green
pigment is visible
through the pictorial layer.

In embarking on the visit of the fresco cycle in the Convent, I believe one must have the cognitive tools necessary for seeing the most salient passages in Angelico's linguistical evolution.

Those elements that help distinguish the most poetic and creative moments from the more repetitive and narrative, whether they flow from the *maestro*'s brush or that of one of his assistants.

In summary, one of the most plausible hypotheses for the development of the cycle seems to be: Angelico had already begun to paint the frescoes in the cells on the East Corridor in 1437 just after the construction of the dormitory.

He painted the frescoes on the outer wall almost entirely by himself, immediately followed by those on the inner wall, with increasing help from collaborators. Work was probably interrupted until the other two dormitories were completed, or until about 1441-1442. At that time, Angelico painted the frescoes on the Ground Floor, and continued the frescoes in the cells until 1443, with assistants, including Benozzo Gozzoli taking a principle, but not exclusive, role.

The second phase of the work began with the cell depicting *Noli me tangere*, and even though it is part of the East Corridor cells, it structurally belongs to the North Corridor wing where we find stylistic similarities to the *Annunciation* and to *Christ on the Cross adored by Saint Dominic* painted on the walls of that corridor.

Lastly, and perhaps still before 1445, the last fresco was painted depicting the *Madonna delle Ombre* in the dormitory of the Clerics.

Madonna delle Ombre,
detail of Saints
John the Evangelist,
Thomas Aquinas and Lawrence;
Corridor of the Clerics, right side.

Ground Floor

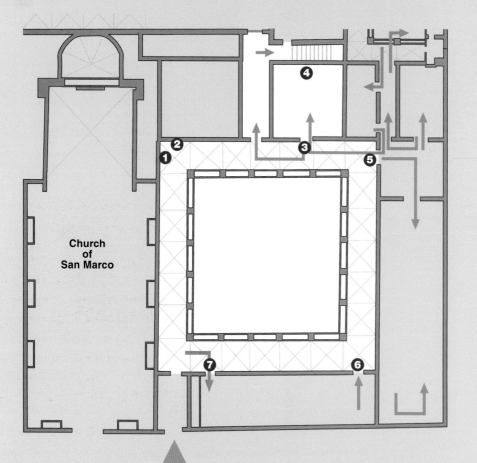

Plan of the Ground Floor

Church of San Marco

1
2
3
4
5
6
7

Frescoes by Fra Angelico on the Ground Floor:

1. Saint Peter of Verona

2. Christ on the Cross adored by Saint Dominic

3. Saint Dominic *(sinopia)*

4. Crucifixion and Saints *(Chapter Room)*

5. Pietà

6. Christ the Pilgrim received by two Dominicans

7. Saint Thomas Aquinas

Plan of the Upper Floor

39
38 40 41 42 43 44
A B
36 35 34 33 32 31 1
37 33a 32a 30 2
29 3
28 4
27 5
26 C 6
25 7
24 8
23 9
14 13 15 16 17 18 19 20 21 22 10
12 11

Frescoes by Fra Angelico on the Upper Floor, except for the Cells of Savonarola 12-14:

A. Annunciation

B. Saint Dominic embracing the Cross

C. Madonna delle Ombre

Cloister of Sant'Antonino

THE VISIT BEGINS WITH the Cloister of Sant'Antonino, just off the entrance to the Museum, where the traditional entrance to the Convent was located.

The fresco of *Christ on the Cross adored by Saint Dominic* stands out on the wall in front of the entrance, framed by a marble moulding made in around 1628, when Cecco Bravo painted the lateral figures of the Virgin and Saint John. This work announces the program for the entire cycle of frescoes. More precisely, it depicts Saint Dominic embracing the cross, with his firm, intense expression demonstrating his sorrow and love for the Crucifix. It synthesises the sense of Dominican piety and underlines the very close bond to Christ and his suffering upon which Dominic based his life and the life of his Order, and which all are called to follow. The intense emotion of this silent dialogue between Saint Dominic and Christ is an invitation to follow in the founder's footsteps and to relive his experiences.

This is the perfect synthesis of the new, measured naturalism, uncovering the soul's deepest impulses in the delicate exploration of the forms of the human body. The symbolic abstraction, realised by extrapolating the figures from any real context and isolating them in space without time, the mental space approaching the surreal and heightened by the intense azurite ground, represents one of Angelico's most masterful moments. The light realistically models the faces of Saint Dominic and Christ, fully capturing their natural expressiveness, and is completely Renaissance in

On pages 22-23: view of the Cloister of Sant' Antonino.

character. Technically, this result is obtained by correctly calibrating the figures in space, using proportional harmony, careful drawing and a perfect mastery of the pictorial technique. All these factors have contributed to the fresco's reasonably good condition, even though located under an open loggia. The areas of greatest deterioration are along the bottom of the fresco, susceptible to the transmigration of the salts in the mortar and masonry. Originally, the power behind this image was strengthened by the stark white walls around it, at the time completely devoid of the frescoes added during the 1600s. There were only the five small lunettes painted by Angelico, over the doors to the rooms facing the Cloister, depicting figures or scenes referencing the function of each room.

To the left of *Christ on the Cross adored by Saint Dominic*, above the door leading into the church, is the lunette with *Saint Peter of Verona asking for Silence*, and continuing clockwise, we find *Saint Dominic with the Rule and the Staffs* above the Chapter Room door (only the sinopia remains here); *Pietà* above the Sala del Lavabo door; *Christ the Pilgrim received by two Dominicans* over the door leading to the Pilgrim's Hospice; *Saint Thomas Aquinas* above the door leading to the old Theology School.

These frescoes, powerful icons visually 'calling to order' some of the most important passages of the Rule, are still relevant as symbolic images even in their deteriorated state.

The most intense image, and the best preserved of

Lunette with the Pietà*; Cloister of Sant'Antonino.*

Right: Christ on the Cross adored by Saint Dominic; *Cloister of Sant'Antonino.*

the series is *Saint Peter of Verona asking for Silence.* The figure forcefully emerges from a background that is only legible in its preparatory state, without the azurite pigment. Its force remains present thanks to the highly plastic, modelled body, the spatial perspective given to the hands, the halo placed in front of the frame, and the painted shadows cast from the frame still visible on the thin, first layer of plaster, the *arriccio.*

Saint Dominic with the Rule and the Staffs, at the entrance to the Chapter Room is reduced to only a shadow of the original, removed from the wall using the *strappo* technique and transferred inside. However, the solid volumes can still be seen in the *sinopia,* one of the rare examples of Angelico's synthetic and incisive drawing.

Above the door to the Sala del Lavabo, just before the Refectory, another fresco has been removed using the *strappo* technique, and is now barely visible. It depicts the anguished image of the *Pietà,* an allusion to the need to nourish ourselves with Him in order to attain eternal life. It is stylistically very similar to the large *Crucifixion* just a few steps away.

The two fresco images on the south side are totally different in tone. They testify to the painter's expressive versatility and technique in adapting the work to its purpose. An old *strappo* transferred onto canvas, *Christ the Pilgrim received by two Dominicans,* is rich in emotion, affection and charity, while the *Saint Thomas Aquinas,* highest authority in Dominican doctrine, remains iconic and slightly outmoded in its capably constructed space.

Above: Lunette with Saint Peter of Verona asking for Silence*;*

Below: Lunette with Saint Thomas Aquinas*;* Cloister of Sant'Antonino.

Lunette with Christ the Pilgrim
received by two Dominicans*;*
Cloister of Sant'Antonino.

Chapter Room

ANGELICO PAINTED THE MOST MONUMENTAL FRESCO of the cycle in the Chapter Room. It depicts the *Crucifixion with Saints* and is enclosed in a frame containing prophetic figures, with a lower row portraying the most illustrious personages in the Dominican Order. In the arched frame, richly decorated with foliage motifs, eight hexagonal windows contain Biblical figures: Daniel, Zechariah, Jacob, David, Isaiah, Jeremiah, Ezechiel, and Job, a mystical theologian, Dionysius the Areopagite, and the pagan prophetess, the Erythraean Sibyl. At the top of the arch, the pelican nourishing its young with its blood is a symbol of redemption, but also of penitence and solitude as evidenced by the inscription (*Psalm* 101, 7-8).

The iconographical scheme in the frame follows a well-established tradition, used also in the frieze of the Porta della Mandorla of the Cathedral. The image in the main scene, however, is completely new. The painter has minimised the presence of historical figures; the Virgin is supported by John, Mary of Cleophas and Mary Magdalene, but along with them in a chorus of meditation, there are the founding fathers of the Order and promoters of the apostolate on the right. On the left there are the patron saints of the city, the convent and the Medici family. Saint John the Baptist, patron saint of Florence, stands in front of the cross of the Good Thief. He is prophet and precursor of Christ, and here, he gestures towards the Saviour, in fulfilment of prophecy. In front of him the Evangelist Mark points to the passage in his Gospel dealing with the prophecy

Crucifixion with Saints,
Chapter Room.

of John. Further to the left, there are the martyr-saints of the Medici: Lawrence with the grate upon which he was martyred, and the two brothers who were physicians (*medici*), Cosmas and Damian. On the right, behind Saint Dominic kneeling in ecstatic prayer, is a group of saints called to represent the model of meditation and of life. Three Doctors and Fathers of the Church who guided Dominic can be identified: Augustine and Ambrose, who asserted Christ's dual human and divine nature, gesture as they look towards the Lord. Saint Jerome is portrayed as a humble penitent, next to him the cardinal's hat, attribute as Doctor of the Church; all promoters of a life dedicated to charity, humility and poverty. They are followed by the founders and reformers of the principle Monastic Orders: Benedict in a black habit; Romuald, founder of the Camaldolese Order, in a white garment; Francis founder of the Friars Minor; Bernard of Clairvaux reformer of the Cistercian Order, and John Gualberto founder of the Vallombrosans. To the very far right are Peter of Verona, martyr, and Thomas Aquinas, Doctor of the Order, portrayed with a particularly penetrating expression, a method used by the artist to synthesise the significance of the Crucifixion as the path to salvation. This path goes directly from the cross down to Saint Dominic, portrayed in the medallion directly below the cross, in a symbolic branching out to the entire Dominican family. On either side, the most illustrious and important Dominican personages are placed in hierarchical order. Next to Dominic are two popes, Innocent V and Benedict XI, the cardinals Hugh of St-Cher and Giovanni Dominici, followed by more or less

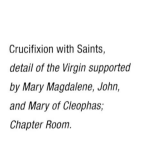

Crucifixion with Saints,
detail of the Virgin supported
by Mary Magdalene, John,
and Mary of Cleophas;
Chapter Room.

Crucifixion with Saints,
detail of Saint John the Baptist;
Chapter Room.

well-known figures among the sainted and beatified.

The composition extends linearly, in a slow, undulating rhythm underlining the enunciative function of the fresco, erasing any narrative or dramatic finality. The placement of the figures in space is characterised by blocks of colour and a palette rich in pure tonalities, delicate and refined, fruit of a masterly use of ochres, earths and lime white, hallmarks of Angelico's frescoes. The painted rendering of the figures is based on very sure drawing, thin, lightly fused brushstrokes and a soft *chiaroscuro* that defines the modelling with extreme delicacy and transparency, typical of the *maestro*'s technique. The faces follow traditional iconography but with new emphasis directed towards the portrayal and the psychological aspects of the individuals, rendering them even more understandable: the intensely mystical expression of Saint Francis, Saint Augustine lost in though, or the enraptured face Saint Peter of Verona.

There is a more graphically explicit and realistic line in the figures in the arched frame, suggesting the intervention of a collaborator, traditionally identified as Benozzo Gozzoli. Other painters seem to have collaborated on the portraits of the Dominicans on the bottom row, most of which however, were executed by Angelico. Due to the loss of the azurite that originally covered the background, flaked or scraped away over the centuries, the general effect and, and most importantly, the spatial effects are notably altered. The blue pigment probably went from a very dark to a very light colour, as indicated by the different tonalities seen in the ground layer, going from white on the horizon to dark red on the top, and probably giving a sense of depth to the scene, which today can only be imagined.

The very few traces of azurite still remaining were uncovered under an old repainting made with red paint during the restoration treatments carried out between 1968 and 1974. That particular restoration is basic to the history of this fresco, not only for the scientific discoveries made, but most importantly, for the level of conservation attained. In 1968, the fresco showed severe signs of sulphate damage that disrupted the adhesion of the plaster-pigments. This had led to the disintegration of the surface, thus putting the survival of the fresco at risk. The need to save the work stimulated the creation of a method of consolidating it while the fresco remained on the wall, and this method has been used in similar situations ever since. The sulphates are chemically transformed into carbonates, re-establishing the cohesion in the pictorial layers and avoiding a *strappo* removal of the fresco from the wall.

Crucifixion with Saints,
detail of Saints Benedict
(black habit), Bernard,
reformer of the Cistercians
(white garment) and Francis,
founder of the Friars Minor;
Chapter Room.

Upper
Floor

Preceding pages:
Annunciation, *detail*
of the Angel of Annunciation;
North Corridor-Corridor
of the Lay Brothers.

Annunciation,
detail if the small window
in the Virgin's room.

Following pages:
Annunciation, *full view.*

North Corridor-Corridor of the Lay Brothers: *Annunciation*

THE STAIRCASE LEADING to the Upper Floor opens onto the corridor of the north dormitory, housing the lay brothers and non-religious guests. At the landing, we find ourselves in front of the *Annunciation*, a fresco fixed in our collective image-depository as the symbol of Angelico's art. It is one of three paintings on the corridor walls, and was probably painted when the construction on the upper floor was underway, and at the same time, or at the end of the work on the frescoes on the Ground Floor, all having notable stylistic similarities.

Angelico conceived the scene as a vision seen through an imaginary window enclosed within an architrave, a sill and a jamb in *faux* stone, suggested, at least on a theoretical level, by Leon Battista Alberti in *De Pictura*. The scene seems to be an extension of real space, a loggia looking onto a garden, very similar to the one just constructed by Michelozzo on the Ground Floor of the Convent, or the one at the Ospedale degli Innocenti by Filippo Brunelleschi.

By demolishing the boundary between the present and a distant past, the artist emotionally involves the viewer in the mystery of the Incarnation.

Angelico had already used the loggia as a setting for the Annunciation in some of his panel paintings, and it is an architectural space familiar to convent life.

A careful study of the architectural composition (Morachiello) reveals that the architecture and the perspective plane do not follow the same plan or

ANTE FIGVRAM PRETEREVNDO CAVE NE SILEATVR AVE

adhere to any hard and fast rules. They were only meant to depict a plausible, pleasant environment where the two figures and their interchange could be effectively framed. Both figures are portrayed in an attitude fully submissive to a greater will. The Virgin sits on a simple stool, alluding to her humility, and is illuminated by two light sources. There is a light that comes from the exterior, from the garden, separated from the woods by a fence creating an *hortus conclusus*. The other light comes from the small window in her room, similar to a cell in a convent, and convergence point for the compositional perspective.

The Latin inscription painted in gold letters on the floor, translated as 'Hail, O Mother of piety and noble domicile of the Holy Trinity', underlines an aspect that surely the fresco was meant to convey: Mary's importance as the heavenly example of charity, the charity that allows her to offer her body so that the Incarnation could be realised, and so Redemption is made possible.

Thus, Mary is the model for humility, charity and love, all the virtues that were constant objectives for the Dominicans. The other inscription painted in black letters on the sill, invites the viewer to always pray to the Virgin when passing in front of the fresco.

The image transmits a spiritual dimension that finds expression in the formal simplicity, in the rarefied atmosphere, in the slow and metered rhythm, in the technique employed.

Pictorial ability was very important in fulfilling Angelico's visual and spiritual objectives. The elements that contribute to the success of the image include a sublime expressive quality created by the use of colour, transparency, fluid drawing, modulations in the luminosity of the drapery – as in the Angel's robe, its soft folds hiding an ethereal yet real body. The search for ultimate spirituality does not hinder the artist in depicting the human body, even if a sacred body, rationally and concretely constructed according to the precepts of the time.

The reason why Mary's dress is devoid of pigment is not known, however the quickly drawn lines of the underdrawing on the plaster are visible. Perhaps the pigment was applied *a secco* and it fell off, or perhaps it was never applied. The gold on the haloes and on the Angel's garment confirm the semi-public location for this work, in a corridor where external visitors – albeit selected – would pass in order to use the Library, and where Cosimo de' Medici's private cell was located.

Annunciation,
detail of the Angel's garment.

View of the East Corridor-
Corridor of the Clerics
and the corner going
to the North Corridor-
Corridor of the Lay Brothers,
with the Annunciation *on the wall.*

East Corridor-Corridor of the Clerics

THE EAST CORRIDOR, ALSO KNOWN AS the Corridor of the Clerics, is to the left of the *Annunciation*. The clerics were the elderly friars, for whom the first twenty cells were built in 1437, and from where the fresco cycle begins.

Each fresco represents an episode in the *Story of Christ*, almost always depicting Saint Dominic, the Virgin, or another one of the Dominican saints, onlookers to the scene. These figures served as intermediaries between the Dominican friar who lived in the cell and Jesus Christ. Based on the artist's plan, they functioned as models, even for meditation, and each scene is constructed as if it were a vision of the saint depicted.

The cell was not only for sleeping, but also for meditation and individual prayer. The key to reading the iconographical text in both the friars' and novices' cells is found in the daily life of the Order. Still missing, however, is the key for understanding the criteria behind the scenes, in no apparent chronological sequence, and it is not clear if there is a connection between these and the underlying program.

There are various hypotheses formulated by scholars, and questions still remain unanswered. One of the most plausible interpretations (Hood) is that the subjects illustrate the passages in the *Synoptic Gospels* from the *Golden Legend* to the *Meditationes vitae Christi*, corresponding to the main feasts of the Dominican liturgical calendar. Others (Madigan, Morachiello) suggest that the frescoes follow an abbreviated structure of the rosary – Marian prayer in the thirteenth century – with references to the main joyful, sorrowful and glorious mysteries. Recently (Morachiello, Spike) identified three subdivided groups in the three fundamental moments of the Salvation: the Birth, the Passion-Death, and the Resurrection following the Scholastic system of logic. Nonetheless, the identification is not strictly linear.

It is generally agreed, however, that almost all the frescoes in the cells on the outer wall, beginning in conventional, numerical order, are the work of Angelico, with rare interventions by some of his collaborators. The intervention of collaborators increases for those cells on the inside wall, until they replace completely the *maestro's* intervention. Angelico however, remains the author of the drawing and probably the *sinopia* on the layer of *arriccio* plaster.

The oldest group of frescoes begins with the *Lamentation over the Dead Christ* in Cell 2. It is probable that the first fresco – *Noli me tangere* – in Cell 1 (Boskovits) dates from a later period, contemporary with the *Annunciation* in the North Corridor (Corridor of the Lay Brothers). Both these later works seem to have stylistic, as well as physical affinities, and being on the northern wing of the building, not finished before 1441.

East Corridor, Outer wall
Cells 1-11

Interior of Cell 1.

Cell 1 – *Noli me tangere*

THE TEXT OF THE GOSPEL ACCORDING to John is instantly synthesised and translated in this fresco. It depicts the apparition of the resurrected Christ to Mary Magdalene, after she discovers the empty tomb: 'When she had thus said, she turned around, and saw Jesus standing there; and she knew not that it was Jesus.'

The fresco seems to make these words come alive, and Mary's gesture of astonishment and Jesus' uncertainty capture the sense of the apparition. The subsequent Gospel passages are also condensed in this one image. The hoe that Jesus carries on his left shoulder tangibly justifies Mary's supposition: 'She, thinking it was the gardener, said to him…'

Her face is painted with surprise and astonishment, reflecting her sentiments upon hearing the stranger call her by name. Mary's outstretched arms capture her desire to detain Jesus, while his right hand makes his refusal clear: 'Do not touch me, for I am not yet ascended to the Father.'

There are a number of ways the artist transmits the emotional sense of the apparition and the extraordinary character of the event: the concentration of the colours, the unreal, apparently awkward construction of the Christ figure, the contrast between the naturalistic and symbolic aspects, the light.

Christ's apparition takes place in a luxuriant garden where all the descriptive elements – the white and red flowers in the grass, the fence in the background, the enclosed cypress, palm and olives trees – contextually respond to the naturalistic as well as symbolic needs.

The splendid red ochre colour of Mary Magdalene's garments attracts and holds our attention. She is bathed in a special light that emanates from above; the light of grace illuminating the first witness to the Resurrection; a light that has nothing to do with the light intrinsic in the candidly white garments and brilliant halo of Jesus Christ.

Although the figure of Jesus seems a bit uncertain in the drawing, and it is painted in a more descriptive manner, the composition and splendid chromatic values in this fresco would make it difficult to attribute it to anyone other than Angelico, responsible for its concept and execution, notwithstanding Hood's recent proposal giving the work to Benozzo Gozzoli.

Noli me tangere, *detail of Mary Magdalene's garment.*

Noli me tangere

Lamentation over the Dead Christ,
detail of a holy woman.

Cell 2 – *Lamentation over the Dead Christ*

THE ASTONISHED FIGURE OF SAINT DOMINIC emerges from the left of the barren rocks that encircle the grotto housing Jesus' Sepulchre, flanked by the outlines of the unreal grey trees with red blossoms. He seems to be meditating on the scene before him: the compassionate care given to Christ's body just removed from the Cross.

The wise choice of dazzling colours, the extraordinary combination of pink, dark red and orange in the garments worn by the holy women and Jospeh of Arimathea, serve to fix our attention on their figures rather than on the lifeless body of Christ.

This explains the thin, diaphanous body, barely modelled, precariously supported on the knees of the Holy Women.

Jesus and Saint Dominic are the only figures where the pathos of the scene is slackened and the only ones that can justify any doubts about the authorship of the fresco.

The rest of the pictorial work cannot be attributed to even the most capable assistant; only a master's hand can convey the emotional intensity on the faces of the mourners and the dense physical presence of their figures, intent on one of the most meaningful moments in Christian charity: preparing Christ's body for entombment; the same charity that was one of the fundamental principles of for the Order set out by Saint Dominic.

Lamentation over the Dead Christ

Cell 3 – *Annunciation*

OF ALL THE CELL FRESCOES, this is the best known. Looking at it, it seems to be a snapshot made in a corner of the cloister in the convent of San Marco. That is where the friars who lived in this cell were to have imagined the scene. The Dominicans were called to reflect upon the extraordinary moment of the Incarnation of Jesus, and consequently the salvation of mankind, following the spiritual example of one of their first martyrs, Peter of Verona, who appears in prayer just outside the scene.

The scene seems to echo the reduced space of the loggia in the Cloister of the Spesa, and helps to intensify the spiritual meeting between the Angel and the Virgin whose slight figure is pervaded by the Angel's light. Their arms are crossed over their breasts, indicating that Mary has already answered the announcement, accepting the will of the Lord (Lk. 1, 35, 38), while the Angel pays silent homage. The two figures are slender and ethereal, set within a virtual arch that unites them, and multiplies *ad infinitum* the shape of the vaults in the loggia. In their simplicity, in their gesture and expression, they illustrate the other primary virtue Saint Dominic wanted to communicate to his followers: Humility.

Here, again, every descriptive detail, every ornamentation that could distract the viewer from reflecting on the 'mystery' has been eliminated by the artist. Once more, the palette is limited to five colours, increasing the concentrated effect of the image. Contributing to this effect is the absence of the blue pigment that, as is customary, should have coloured the Virgin's mantle. Rather than damaged, the garment was most likely left unfinished, and today it can be seen in its preparatory stage. The outline of the drawing is made with olive green paint, and the drapery folds are modelled with red sinopia, offering outstanding testimony to the procedure and technique used in Angelico's wall paintings.

Annunciation,
detail of the Virgin's mantle.

Annunciation

Cell 4 – *Crucifixion with the Virgin and Saints John the Evangelist, Dominic and Jerome*

THIS IS PROBABLY THE FIRST CRUCIFIXION painted for the cells, and its iconographical scheme will be used again and again in the others. The black sky in the background, faithfully following the evangelical account – 'It was now about noon and darkness came over the whole land until three in the afternoon because of the eclipse of the sun' – emphasises the Cross and the slender body with its flanks wrapped in a white loincloth. The transparency of the cloth flutters against the darkness of the sky, an elegant remnant, along with the naked, craggy rocks at the sides of the Cross, part of Late Gothic culture.

Here, placed at the foot of the Cross with the Virgin and Saint John are two other chosen witnesses: next to the usual figure of Saint Dominic in prayer, is Saint Jerome from whom the first monastic institutions descend. He is dressed as a hermit, with a book, a scourge and a cardinal's hat at his feet. All the figures are endowed with the calm melancholy typical of Angelico, purified by the serenity that comes from the certainty of the Resurrection and salvation expressed on the face of Christ.

The compositional balance, the very high quality of the work consistent with the other frescoes, the similar technique and the synthetic composition dispel any doubts, advanced by some scholars, about its authorship.

Crucifixion with the Virgin
and Saints John the Evangelist,
Dominic and Jerome,
detail of Saint Dominic.

Crucifixion with the Virgin and Saints John the Evangelist, Dominic and Jerome

The Nativity, *detail*
of Saint Catherine of Alexandria.

Cell 5 – *The Nativity*

THE FRESCO, DOMINATED BY THE OVER-SIZED STRAW hut built in front of a grotto, is centred around the Infant Jesus, lying on a bit of straw on the ground. He is delicate and fragile, the personification of innocence and humility, but the importance of his coming into the world is revealed by the light surrounding him, a strong warm light, and even though coinciding with the source of natural light from the right, surpasses all reality.

The analogy with the Gospel according to John is clear (Jn. 1, 9): 'The true light, which enlightens everyone, was coming into the world.' All present in the scene are illuminated by this light: Joseph, Mary, the two chosen witnesses in the fresco, Saint Catherine of Alexandria and Saint Peter of Verona, kneeling at the extremities of the imaginary diagonal running through the scene.

The soft modelling on the figures, very close to the type found in the *Lamentation over the Dead Christ*, the rhythmic separation in the composition, the chromatic range and the painting technique lead again to Angelico, an attribution contested in the past by some scholars.

The only uncontested exception is seen in the angels above, whose fairly indulgent execution betrays an intervention by one of Angelico's collaborators.

The Nativity

Cell 6 – *Transfiguration*

'AFTER SIX DAYS JESUS TOOK Peter, James, and John his brother, and led them up a high mountain by themselves. And he was transfigured before them. And his face shone like the sun and his garments became white as light. And behold, there appeared to them Moses and Elijah talking with him' (Mt. 17, 1-3).

The fresco fully expresses the sense of the disturbing vision experienced by Peter, James and John, taken by Jesus to Mount Tabor in Galilee.

This unworldly sense is due not only to their gestures and the enraptured expressions of the three disciples, but especially the surreal dimension of the scene, without a background, a setting or the realistic elements in the compositional structure.

The figures are bathed in a cascade of light that washes out their colour, removing them from any real context. They encircle Jesus Christ who rises on the rock with arms spread open, prefiguring his crucifixion.

In the space encircling Christ, together with the disciples it seems natural to find Moses and Elijah, appearing in the clouds. There are also the Virgin and Saint Dominic in prayer meditating on the mystery. Through the masterful use of fresco technique, the artist depicts the atmospheric transparency and the light itself.

He begins with the purest tonality in the figure of Christ, and it progressively becomes warmer and richer, transforming its supernatural quality into natural, solar light.

The monumental figure of Christ, his solemn expression of tranquil resolution, fully translate the meaning of the words 'listen to him' – God's invitation to the disciples, which every Dominican brother was called to follow.

Transfiguration,
detail of Peter, the disciple.

Transfiguration

Cell 7 – Mocking of Christ with the Virgin and Saint Dominic

THIS IS ONE OF THE FRESCOES where the artist reaches the height of symbolic abstraction. This aspect is already embodied in the primary role played by the two witnesses, the Virgin and Saint Dominic, the intermediaries between humanity and divinity, placed in the foreground on a pink terrace that separates and raises them off the ground. Behind them, on a third plane, physically set off by the white colour, is the scene depicting Christ being mocked after his arrest.

The event is comprised of a series of acts, amply described in the Gospel according to Matthew: 'They stripped off his clothes and put a scarlet military cloak on him. Weaving a crown out of thorns, they placed it on his head, and put a reed in his right hand. And kneeling before him, they mocked him saying, "Hail, King of the Jews". They spat upon him and took the reed, striking him on the head.' (Mt. 27, 28-29).

All the sequences in Matthew's account, as well as the blows related in John's text (Jn. 19, 2-3) are concentrated into a single synchronic image, inspired by the iconographical elements in the *Imagines Pietatis*, where the persons and the instruments of the passion were synthetically and symbolically depicted next to Christ rising from the tomb. Here, Christ is depicted differently from the Gospel descriptions. He wears the white garment that, according to the *Golden Legend*, was given to him in the house of Herod, and he supports the derision inflicted upon him with regal dignity.

Even the choice of colours is symbolically significant: the black sky behind the praetorial wall, the red seat alluding to mocked regality, the green cloth behind Jesus evoking the hope in the Resurrection, Christ's white garments symbolising innocence and sacredness.

The most intense passage in the fresco, and one of Angelico's most artistically extraordinary moments, is the face of Saint Dominic executed in the single *giornata* section, painted together with his right hand in only one day.

Compared with this, the figure of the sorrowing Virgin is less incisive, and a few uncertainties in the drawing, point us toward the work of a collaborator, who some scholars identify as the young Benozzo Gozzoli.

Mocking of Christ with the Virgin and Saint Dominic

Cell 8 – *The Holy Women at the Sepulchre*

THE SCENE DEPICTING THE DISCOVERY by the Holy Women of the Resurrection is introduced by Saint Dominic kneeling in the left edge of the fresco, lost in prayerful ecstasy.

As in other works in San Marco, the image synthesises various passages in the Gospel stories, and particular attention is placed on the emotions of each figure. The Holy Women have just entered the grotto where they find Jesus' tomb uncovered.

The Gospels identify the Holy Women as Mary Magdalene, Mary the mother of James, Joanna, according to Luke (Lk. 24, 1-10) and Salome, according to Mark (Mk. 16, 1-7). However, Angelico substituted one of these figures with the Virgin Mary, recognisable by the star on her head.

In a single visual space, the artist depicts the women arriving at the tomb with perfumed oils in hand, the discovery of the empty tomb, the presence and encouraging words of the Angel: 'On entering the tomb they saw a young figure sitting on the right side, clothed in a white robe, and they were afraid. But he said to them, "Do not be afraid! You seek Jesus of Nazareth, the crucified. He has been raised; he is not here. Behold, the place where they laid him."' (Mk. 16, 5-7).

The artist gives visual form to the words of the angel, and the main theme of the fresco is the image of the resurrected Christ in a mandorla of light, holding the banner and the martyr's palm.

As always, Angelico's hand is confirmed in the drawing and a in few of the figures of particularly expressive intensity and pictorial quality, such as Saint Dominic, and the Magdalene depicted with highly effective foreshortening, bent over the empty sepulchre.

The authorship in other parts of the fresco may leave room for doubt. Even though the Angel is faithful to Angelico's type, it is a bit academic in its execution, just as the two Holy Women on the left seem to be less expressive than the one on the right, attributable to the *maestro*. These two figures have a certain affinity with the figure of the Virgin in the previous cell, and could be the work of the same collaborator, identified by some as Benozzo Gozzoli.

The Holy Women at the Sepulchre

The Holy Women at the Sepulchre,
detail of the Angel
and Saint Dominic praying.

Above:
detail of the Magdalene
leaning over the tomb.

Cell 9 – *Coronation of the Virgin*

USING BRUSHSTROKES WITH VERY THINLY washed colour, Angelico has created the effect of the Heavens drenched in colourless light, where Christ pays homage to the mediatrix of the Salvation by crowning her *Regina Coeli*, Queen of Heaven.

Light is everywhere, in the atmosphere, the clouds, the faces, the garments. It saturates and illuminates all the different tonalities of white used unsparingly by the artist to reinforce the divine, unworldly quality of the scene.

Unlike Angelico's panel paintings of the *Coronation* (in the Louvre, the San Marco Museum and the Uffizi) which were meant to strike the imagination of the populace, here, there is no show of glory,

power, sovereignty. The act of placing the crown on Mary's head has no triumphant gesture. She bends over to receive the crown and folds her arms to her breast with the same humility as in the Annunciation.

Humility, admiration, acceptance, prayer are expressed by the common gesture of all the other figures united in an unreal circle, in radiant contemplation of the image above them.

For the brother who lived in this cell, the presence of Dominic and Francis, Benedict and Peter of Verona, Thomas Aquinas and Mark the Evangelist, all called together in witness of their faith, obedient and devoted to Christ and Mary in a symbolic communion of saints and apostles, was an invitation for harmony and concord even in convent life.

Coronation of the Virgin,
detail of Saint Francis.

Coronation of the Virgin

Cell 10 – *Presentation in the Temple*

THIS IS ONE OF THE MOST HIGHLY praised frescoes in the entire cycle. The temple where the ceremony takes place is represented by a few, simple architectural elements, masterfully defined with gradations of white pigment, modulating to grey in the shadows. The spatial definition is obtained by the simple pictorial construction of the apse wall carefully lit from the right. It is decorated with a shell motif, partially recovered as a result of a restoration treatment that removed the red overpaint covering the entire background, and until the upper part of the painted vault was demolished at some unknown point in time, must have continued further on in space. The classical architectural motif echoes the taste of the times and was particularly dear to Michelozzo, the architect who constructed the convent, and with whom Angelico was in constant rapport.

Before the altar the young mother Mary, apprehensively reaches out toward the Infant Jesus who Simeon cradles in his arms. A band of light is concentrated on the elderly priest's face, whose enraptured gaze expresses his joy. He has known the Messiah, and can now die in peace, as told in the Gospel according to Luke (Lk. 2, 29-35).

Joseph is standing behind Mary, serene and confident, and as prescribed by the Law of Moses, he brings a pair of turtledoves or doves to offer in sacrifice. Standing on the right in profile is the elderly prophetess, Anna, present for the ceremony and to meet the Redeemer. In contemplative meditation of the scene, Saint Peter of Verona is kneeling in the left foreground.

The *Presentation in the Temple* was a particularly important event for the Order, which celebrated the sacred moment on the feast of the Purification of the Blessed Virgin, the 2nd of February.

At the convent of San Marco it was celebrated with songs and nocturnal processions in the cloister. San Marco also hosted the Company of the Purification, for which Angelico had painted a *Banner*, now lost. The theme of offering the Child to the Lord could be easily interpreted as a symbol of offering the young novice to God, the beginning of religious life. The presence of this fresco in the wing of the dormitory reserved to the novices is thus explained, and this was probably the prior's cell.

Presentation in the Temple

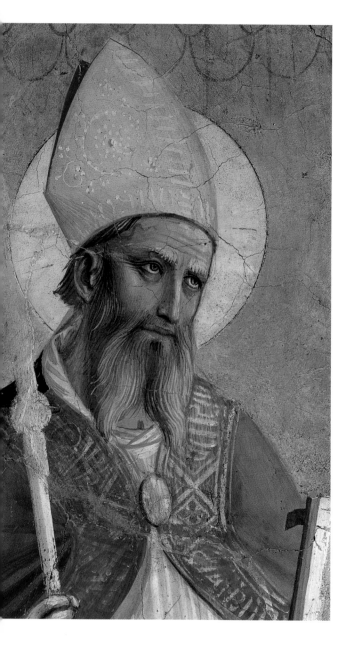

The Madonna and Child
enthroned between Saints
Augustine and Thomas,
detail of Saint Augustine.

Cell 11 – *The Madonna and Child enthroned between Saints Augustine and Thomas*

THE IMAGE OF THIS FRESCO EXPRESSES the institutional foundations of the Dominican Order. It has been compared to a wood panel triptych depicting the individuals who preside over the life and Rule of the Order. However, in this Renaissance version, the straight-on presentation of the figures has disappeared in favour of a semi-circular placement, making the interaction between saints and the divine figures more believable.

The Virgin is seated on a throne with a red canopy, while the Christ Child, standing on her knees, holds the globe fairly casually in one hand and blesses with the other. Next to them Saint Augustine and Saint Thomas (interpreted by some as Saint Dominic), with indulgent expressions, are holding the Summa and the Rule. The fresco is in one of the two cells reserved for the prior, and synthesises his didactic role in the community.

The fresco is generally agreed to be by one of Angelico's assistants, however, because of the confidently executed proportions, the spatial presentation and the intensity of the workmanship, Saint Augustine's cloak, painted in only one day, can be attributed to the *maestro*. The central group is most certainly by the same collaborator who painted the angels in the *Nativity*. Here, Angelico's usual placement is repeated, but this time with minimal effect, and Saint Thomas is much less meaningful and more affected than usual.

The Madonna and Child enthroned between Saints Augustine and Thomas

Crucifixion with Saint Dominic in prayer

South Corridor-Corridor of the Novices
Cells 21-15

BEFORE LOOKING AT THE FRESCOES in the cells situated along the internal wall of the East Corridor, it is best to go on to the last corridor, running along the south side of the complex, where the seven largest cells, those reserved for the novices, are located.

Each of these cells has a fresco with a seemingly repetitive shape and subject: the *Crucifixion with Saint Dominic in prayer*. The stylistic and compositional prototype is found in the fresco by Angelico at the beginning of the Corridor of the Clerics depicting *Saint Dominic embracing the Cross*. Each of these seven frescoes, however, depicts Saint Dominic in a different pose, corresponding to the various ways of praying that were practised and recommended by the saint.

Thus, these frescoes have a specific didactic purpose for each brother occupying the cell, all of whom where novices, and during the year of study prior to profession into the Order had to become accustomed to prayer, assisted by an association between state of mind and position of the body.

The model is described, both in writing and visually illuminated in some versions, in the tract called *De modo orandi*, edited by a brother from Bologna during the second half of the thirteenth century. At the time, the small booklet was in circulation as an appendix to the *Life of Saint Dominic*, and many of its ideas are gathered from a treatise on education drafted in the twelfth century by Hugh of St. Victor, annotator on the Augustinian Rule. The tract illustrated eight ways of praying before the Crucifix combining the emotions with the positions of the body. It was well known in the *Quattrocento* among the Dominicans, and Saint Antonino refers to it in the third part of his *Cronaca*.

The image of the Crucifixion depicted by the frescoes is totally removed from context, and is not meant to describe the event. The Crucifix stands out on the white plaster background as if it were a drawing on a page of a manuscript. The frame around the fresco (original in the last cell, number 15) is also reminiscent of an illuminated page. The artist creates the mental image of the Crucifix that each brother had within, along with the image of Saint Dominic, at times depicted in his youth, at times older, in the different positions and attitudes traditionally prescribed.

In the first cell – number 21 – Saint Dominic prays

Crucifixion with Saint Dominic in prayer

Crucifixion with Saint Dominic in prayer

Crucifixion with Saint Dominic in prayer

with open arms, as prescribed by the sixth method of praying, meant to implore God's help in an exceptional task. The second cell, number 20, shows the saint in self-flagellation, and even though Dominic used this practice also in solitude, in the Order it was only allowed in the collective assembly of the Chapter.

Cell 19, the third cell, depicts the saint holding a book in his right hand and with his left shows the intensity of emotion possible by prayer accompanied by studies of the Holy Scripture and meditation on the Crucifixion, as described in the eighth method.

There is no method that corresponds exactly to the arms crossed over the chest as depicted in the fourth cell, number 18. It seems to be a variation on the first method of praying, a lowering ofthe body.

In the fifth cell, number 17, Saint Dominic's hands are intertwined, the most common attitude in prayer, which refers to the fifth method, meditation.

Cell 16, the sixth cell, depicts Saint Dominic embracing the Cross in the same gesture used in the large fresco in the Cloister, and the one in the North Corridor near the stairs. There is a similar gesture in *De modo orandi* that synthesises the level of intensity required in all prayer, and it was obviously preferred by Angelico and his brethren.

The last cell, number 15, shows Saint Dominic with his hands joined together and his eyes turned upwards to the Crucifix. This attitude belongs to the gestures leading to ecstasy, described in the seventh method of praying.

The frescoes are stylistically close to Angelico, and even though they are very high quality, cannot be given to the *maestro*. They appear to be by an able artist under the master's close guidance.

The figures are always well constructed, but the drawing is minute, descriptive, less essential than Angelico. The modelling is characterised by unexpected touches of light and audacious foreshortening, usually much more controlled in Angelico's work.

All these elements indicate Benozzo Gozzoli, commonly agreed upon by scholars, as the painter for these frescoes. The last ones were probably painted just before 1443 or at the latest 1444, when Benozzo began work with Lorenzo Ghiberti on the Baptistery Doors.

East Corridor, Internal wall – Cells 22-30

ONCE THE VISIT TO THE SOUTH CORRIDOR is complete, with the three end rooms at one time the Vestry, converted towards the end of the 1400s into the chapel, study and cell of Fra Girolamo Savonarola, we return to the East Corridor to view the frescoes in the cells on the left wall overlooking the Cloister.

The frescoes in the cells on this side of the corridor repeatedly depict the scenes from the *Crucifixion*, different from one another only by the presence and actions of the onlookers. They are alternated by other episodes from the life of Christ: the *Baptism*, the *Rising from the Sepulchre*, at the *Christ at the Column*, the *Road to Calvary*, in a chronological order that is still difficult to interpret.

Cell 22 – *Crucifixion with the Sorrowing Virgin*

CONCEPTUALLY, ICONOGRAPHICALLY and stylistically this fresco belongs to the series of frescoes in the Novices' cells, and appears to be by the same painter. This cell may have been reserved for the noviciate master, where the presence of the Virgin Mary instead of Saint Dominic indicates her function as role model for the Dominicans, just as Saint Dominic is role model for behaviour and prayer.

The figure of the Virgin cloaked in a lilac-coloured mantle lined in green, even more clearly than the previous frescoes, demonstrates a style different from that of Angelico, especially in relation to the first cells.

Here, the use of colour is different, the drawing is more graphic and conventional in the drapery, the roundness in the face, the sharp highlights and strong contrasts in the facial features, the indifference to spatial problems distance us from the *maestro*. Nonetheless, the generally Angelican effect is pleasing, however here, the master's art is only a superficial echo.

Crucifixion with the Sorrowing Virgin

Cell 23 – *Jesus nailed to the Cross by the Virtues*

THE ICONOGRAPHY OF THE CRUCIFIXION presented in this fresco is fairly unusual, and shows the Virtues hovering around the cross wielding the hammer to drive the nails further into the wood. This representation, quite rare in Italian art, is widely used north of the Alps.

There are twenty known works with this iconography, and only two in Italy: this is one of them. At each side of the Crucifix there are two of the more usual Dominican onlookers, and their presence in this case is clearly didactic: Saint Dominic in prayer and Mary, pointing to Christ while she looks out to the viewer, in her role of intermediary.

From an artistic point of view, the beautiful pictorial quality in the figure of Saint Dominic, his face effectively back-lit and the garments softly draped with great three-dimensional effect, is not present in the entire fresco.

This leads to the hypothesis that Angelico, the author of this figure, was assisted by two collaborators for the other parts. One of these, the artist who painted the Crucifix, is most probably identified as Benozzo Gozzoli, for the exquisitely graphic manner in drawing the figure, analogous to those in the frescoes in the Corridor of the Novices.

Jesus nailed to the Cross by the Virtues, *detail.*

Jesus nailed to the Cross by the Virtues

Cell 24 – *Baptism of Christ*

THE FRESCO IN THIS CELL is completely different in style and composition. The painting of this fresco took longer than usual, as seen by the number of *giornate*, evidenced by the joins in the plaster: five *giornate* for the figures and two for the landscape. For the first time, the landscape takes on new importance and dimension, fading into the horizon and highlighting the appearance of the Holy Spirit, seen as a dove, in concentric circles of light. Even though the figures are faithful to Angelican types, the geometrically linear construction and the barely modelled volumes do not seem to directly refer to the master's style.

The gradual *chiaroscuro* in the modelling is missing, and instead, there are unexpected touches of light and shadow that harden the lines in the face, otherwise graphically correct.

This pictorial style, with a tendency to simplify the lines, is similar to that of Zanobi Strozzi, a faithful imitator and collaborator of Fra Giovanni, and recalled by Giogio Vasari for the illumination work on some of the *Chorals* executed between 1447 and 1454 for the convent of San Marco.

Strozzi could have been responsible for the execution of the main part of this fresco, closely watched over by the *maestro* and perhaps with the help of an assistant, author of the two kneeling angels on the left.

Baptism of Christ,
detail.

Baptism of Christ

Crucifixion with the Virgin, the Magdalene and Saint Dominic

Cell 25 – *Crucifixion with the Virgin, the Magdalene and Saint Dominic*

THE ICONOGRAPHICAL COMPOSITION of this work recalls the Gothic tradition usually followed by Angelico, with the Crucifix between two rocky spurs and placed against a black sky, as stated in the Gospels.

The Magdalene embraces the cross with an impulsive gesture of love and sorrow. The sorrowing Virgin turns towards the viewer, in an invitation to reflect upon the event, and appears almost removed from the scene itself, a symbolic model along with Saint Dominic.

Stylistically, the fresco seems to be fruit of the collaboration of Angelico, author of the beautiful figure of Saint Dominic and perhaps Christ, and an unidentified collaborator, who subserviently follows the *maestro*'s choice of palette, but who is weaker in the drawing and the foreshortening.

Crucifixion with the Virgin,
the Magdalene and Saint Dominic,
detail of Saint Dominic.

Cell 26 – *Christ rising from the Sepulchre, with the Virgin and Saint Thomas (or Saint Dominic?)*

THIS FRESCO HAS A RICHER ICONOGRAPHY than its title may indicate. It contains the symbolic representation of the various phases of the Passion – from Judas' betrayal to Peter's denial, to the mocking of Christ – reproduced in the visual shorthand already used in Cell 7 for the *Mocking of Christ*. The intensity of Mary's expression and the symbols of the Passion – especially Peter's beautifully painted head – are the work of Angelico, while a collaborator is responsible for the figure of the Dominican saint, with pen and book, attributes and facial features that identify Saint Thomas Aquinas, rather than Saint Dominic.

Christ rising from the Sepulchre,
detail of the symbols of the Passion.

Christ rising from the Sepulchre, with the Virgin and Saint Thomas (or Saint Dominic?)

Christ at the Column with the Virgin and Saint Dominic

Cell 27 – *Christ at the Column with the Virgin and Saint Dominic*

THIS FRESCO IS STRONGLY SYMBOLIC and clarifies its didactic function more than in the others. In the foreground are the two figures acting as reference points for the brother contemplating this fresco. On the left, Mary is in the act of requesting grace, while at the same time she accepts a higher will. At the right, Saint Dominic is in the act of flagellating himself, in an attempt at becoming one with Christ's suffering. Their mental vision of Christ's flagellation is made real, including them as participants.

The distinction between reality and imagination is erased, and the link between the viewer and the participants is completed.

Stylistically, there is a notable difference between Mary and Saint Dominic, both modelled with light and colour, and the figure of Christ, simplified, and without true expression. This difference points to the work of a lesser collaborator, perhaps the same artist who painted the Saint Dominic figure in the *Lamentation over the Dead Christ* (Cell 2). The drawing and colour choice in the architecture distances it from Angelico.

Christ at the Column with the
Virgin and Saint Dominic,
detail of Saint Dominic.

Cell 28 – *Road to Calvary with the Virgin and Saint Dominic*

WITH RESPECT TO THE OTHER FRESCOES, this is work is smaller and the figures are not proportionally correct with respect to each other. While both the figures of Saint Dominic and the diaphanous figure of Christ, rich in expressive intensity, seem to be attributable to Angelico, the over-sized, non-homogeneous figure of Mary must be assigned to a collaborator.

Cell 29 – *Crucifixion with the Virgin and Saint Peter of Verona*

ANGELICO IN THIS CASE DELEGATED THE PAINTING, and perhaps even the drawing, to a collaborator. The paint is applied very broadly in some areas, as seen by the large brushstrokes that block in the folds in the Virgin's garments and the structure of the rocks. In other areas there is a dense series of brushstrokes building up the shadows in the faces filled with emotion, coupled with some technical difficulties found in Saint Peter's left hand.

Cell 30 – *Crucifixion with the Virgin and Saint Dominic*

THIS CELL HAS ANOTHER CRUCIFIXION with the sorrowing Virgin, seated on the ground – a solution used by Lorenzo Monaco – with Saint Dominic, his hands joined in a gesture of afflicted ecstasy.

The fresco is of good quality, and because of the descriptiveness in Saint Dominic's detailed face could be associated with Benozzo Gozzoli, while the Virgin and the Crucifix, elegant in line and the transparency of the colours, seem to belong to the hand of Angelico.

Road to Calvary with the Virgin and Saint Dominic

Crucifixion with the Virgin and Saint Peter of Verona

Crucifixion with the Virgin and Saint Dominic

INRI

alue mundi salutare · salue salue Jesu chare · Cruci tue me appare · Velim uere tu scis quare · Presta mihi copiam·

North Corridor-Corridor of the Lay Brothers
Cells nn. 31-43

A T THE END OF THE CORRIDOR OF THE CLERICS, on the wall next to the stairs, there is a fresco depicting *Saint Dominic embracing the Cross*, analogous to the one found in the Cloister upon entering the Convent, and the same image the brothers and novices saw when they left their cells. The symbolic aspect of the scene is strengthened by the absence of a realistic sky, and it seems to be the frontispiece of a prayer book or a Rule of the Order. The image is an invitation to face the day with the knowledge of Christ's love, and with love for Christ, to gather strength from Him in facing the apostolate. The life-giving drops of Christ's blood, source of charity and redemption, flow from his wounds and bathe the ground below. The saint holds onto the cross as if it were a bastion from which he does not want to be separated.

Under the image, on an imitation-stone base, there is an inscription in Latin dating perhaps from the end of the 1400s, with a greeting and a plea for help in emulating the sacrifice of Jesus. The fresco has a superbly material quality, especially the modulations on Saint Dominic's face. It is one of the most beautiful of Angelico's works, and a model for the frescoes in the Cells of the Novices, begun at the same time as the work on the cells in this corridor.

The frescoes in these cells are different from the previous ones in subject, style and destination. The scenes are rich with figures, motion, surroundings. The subjects are all taken from stories of Jesus' life, but now the focus is on the sequence of historical events marking the different events in Christ's Passion, up to the Crucifixion, and not on the emblematic value of the sacred mysteries. The images are no longer used for meditation, but rather, are verses that illustrate the Gospels. The narrative language is easy to understand for even those, who, like the lay brothers who lived in these cells, did not complete studies as did the friars, and who were assigned the humblest tasks in the convent. This narrative function is confirmed by the fact that in the first cells on the inner wall, the Virgin and the Dominican saints are not present, usually the intermediaries for meditation, and they appear only in the last cells with the repeated image of the *Crucifixion*. The visual language is short and abbreviated, and there is greater workshop collaboration, even if the guide for the image is Angelico, perhaps forced to hasten the completion time before the consecration of the Convent in 1443.

No information exists on the identification of the collaborators or their work, at least there is no certainty or clarity about this aspect of the frescoes. There are a number of scholars (Padoa Rizzo, Bonsanti, Morachiello) who would tend to give the collaborators, and especially Benozzo Gozzoli, an ever-greater role in the realisation of the frescoes. Others (Bellosi, Boskovits) would limit intervention by an assistant, and substantially give the entire illustrative cycle to Angelico, explaining the stylistic differences by a different chronology of execution, placing the frescoes in Cells 36-37 and Cells 40-45 in the period 1449-1452 when Angelico returned from Rome, citing the analogies found with his frescoes in that city.

Saint Dominic
embracing the Cross, *full view.*

Cell 31 – *Christ's descent into Hell*

Traditionally, THE FIRST CELL on the left is associated with Saint Antonino, perhaps used as a chapel. The creative idea of this *Descent into Hell* can be attributed only to Angelico. Christ's apparition takes place in a grotto-fortress setting, with the bolt on the door torn way by the force of the divine spirit triumphant over Evil, depicted as a devil crushed under the weight of the door while other devils escape into the crags in the rocks. Christ and the first elderly figure liberated by Jesus have an Angelican imprint, with masterly modulation of tonality in the whites. There are some uncertainties in the definition of Christ's body, similar to the Christ in *Noli me tangere*, leaving open the possibility of intervention by Benozzo Gozzoli, as well as another assistant for the figures in the background, similar to the painting in the *Baptism of Christ*.

Cell 32 – *Sermon on the Mount*

Gathered TOGETHER IN A CIRCLE before him, Jesus speaks to his apostles on the naked rocks of the mountain. The dark halo identifies the traitor, Judas. The circular composition already used by Angelico in other frescoes such as the *Transfiguration* is again repeated. There is a notable difference in the execution of the figures. Some are painted is a very refined manner, using a light, carefully constructed drawing, with classical, regular features. These figures, Christ and the fourth disciple in profile on the right, can be placed in reference to the *maestro* or a highly gifted collaborator. Other figures are painted with rapid lines, a heavily outlined shape and facial features, conventionally executed drapery, minimal *chiaroscuro* in the modelling, and are the work of an assistant.

Cell 32a – *Temptation of Christ*

The FRESCO WAS CUT AWAY when the cell was partially demolished in order to open a window onto the Cloister. The two sequences of this episode take place in the rich landscape extending as far as the eye can see. On the top of the mountain Christ is tempted by and rejects the devil, whose diabolic nature is revealed by his claws and bat-like wings emerging from under his human semblance. Below, the angels offer food to the stately figure of Christ, majestically seated in prayer and wrapped in the soft drapery of a green and lilac-coloured mantle over his pink robe. It is important to note the detail in the fruit and drink the Angel offers to Jesus, a precocious example of still-life painting and a glimpse into daily life. Here there is the same collaboration as in the previous cell between Angelico who painted the beautiful lower section, and an assistant, responsible for the upper area.

Christ's descent into Hell

Sermon on the Mount

Temptation of Christ

Arrest of Christ

Cell 33 – *Arrest of Christ*

THIS FRESCO UNFOLDS IN A SERIES of dramatic events, heightened by alternating tonalities of green, red, and yellow, the movement in Peter's yellow mantle, and the frozen gestures of the figures. The horizontal movement of the scene and the mantle flapping in the wind are traditional devices repeated here with great effect.

The fresco appears to be a collaborative effort. Angelico's hand is apparent in the nobility of the drawn line and careful modelling, as well as in some of the figures such as Christ, the elderly figure on the left, and perhaps the beautiful olive trees growing on the bare rocky hills. One or more assistants worked on the other figures.

Cell 33a – *Entry into Jerusalem*

THIS FRESCO IS ALSO FRAGMENTARY for the same reasons as the painting in Cell 32. Angelico assigned the figures of the apostles to a collaborator, and they are analogous to those depicting the saints in the *Descent into Hell*, most likely identifiable in Zanobi Strozzi.

Entry into Jerusalem

Cell 34 – *Agony in the Garden*

The composition of the fresco is quite unusual. Two different scenes, with two different protagonists are combined together. On the left, Christ is praying in the garden, while the disciples John, Peter and James sleep. The right side opens onto the house of Mary and Martha, Lazarus' sisters, who are intent in prayer. At times, this fresco has been attributed to Benozzo Gozzoli, but the two intense female figures, and in particular Mary's face, inspiration for the face of the Virgin Mary in the Chapter Room *Crucifixion*, point to Angelico's intervention.

The left side of the fresco, however, reveals the same hand as the assistant who painted some of the figures in the *Arrest of Christ*.

Agony in the Garden,
detail of Lazarus' sisters,
Martha and Mary.

Agony in the Garden

Cell 35 – *Institution of the Eucharist*

THE SCENE APPARENTLY SEEMS TO DEPICT the Last Supper. However, the traditional iconography has been changed, transforming the subject in this case into the *Institution of the Eucharist.*

There is no trace of food on the table, and the chalice and paten are emphasised by their size. Christ is offering the broken bread to John: 'Then he took the bread, said the blessing, broke it, and gave it to his disciples saying, "This is my body, which will be given for you; do this in memory of me"' (Lk. 22, 19).

Some of the apostles are seated at the table, while others, including Judas, are kneeling on the right. Kneeling at the left there is even Mary Magdalene. It has been correctly pointed out (Hood) that the scene relates to the feast of the Body and Blood of Christ and is closely parallel to the text in the *Hymns and Hour of Lauds* in the Office of the Feast of the Body and Blood of Christ, written by Saint Thomas Aquinas.

The artist links the event to the Order by staging it in one of the cells in the convent of San Marco.

The execution of the fresco seems to be divided between Angelico, who painted the figure of Christ and the group on the right, and the usual mediocre assistant.

Cell 36 – *Christ nailed to the Cross*

THE FAIRLY UNUSUAL ICONOGRAPHY, seemingly derived from Byzantine sources, was nonetheless known within Franciscan circles because the scene is described textually in the *Meditationes vitae Christi.* The words streaming from Christ's mouth are those related in Luke's Gospel: 'Father, forgive them, they know not what they do' (Lk. 23, 34). This is one of the frescoes where the insistence on reality is paramount, in both the rendering of the objects and the very accentuated physiognomy that point towards the presence of Gozzoli alongside the *maestro*, whose hand can be identified in the group on the right.

Cell 37 – *Crucifixion with Saint John the Evangelist, the Virgin, Saints Dominic and Thomas*

THIS SCENE IS MODELLED on the large *Crucifixion* in the Chapter Room, which could mean that this cell, larger than the others, housed the Chapter for the *fratres conversi*, the Lay Brothers. The fresco has the same abbreviated, simplified style of the assistant encountered frequently in the cells on this side of the corridor.

Institution of the Eucharist

Christ nailed to the Cross

Crucifixion with Saint John the Evangelist, the Virgin, Saints Dominic and Thomas

Cells of Cosimo de' Medici (the Elder)
Cell 38 – *Crucifixion with the Virgin and Saints Cosmas, John, and Peter of Verona*
Cell 39 – *Adoration of the Magi*

THESE TWO FRESCOES MUST BE COMMENTED together because they were made for the cells destined for the benefactor of the convent, Cosimo de' Medici, during his moments of spiritual retreat. In the small cell, the *Crucifixion with the Virgin and Saints Cosmas, John, and Peter of Verona*, is frescoed over a window that has been transformed into a wall closet, closing off the terrace balcony behind it. The cell opens on to a slightly elevated, adjacent room, with a frescoed tabernacle built into the wall, confirming its use as a private oratory, and is placed under a large lunette depicting the *Adoration*

of the Magi. The use of this space by a member of the Medici family is related in the *Cronaca* from the *Quattrocento,* and is confirmed by the iconographical choice and the unusual presence of a costly pigment: the azurite used on the background.

The fresco in the first cell depicts a precise moment of the *Crucifixion,* when Jesus entrusts John to His mother as her adopted son: 'Mulier ecce filius tuus' (Jn. 19, 26-27). Alongside Mary and John, the presence of Cosmas and Peter, patron saints to Cosimo and his son Piero, can be explained (Morachiello) by the desire to involve the two Medici in the newly established parentage between Mary and John through the intercession of their patron saints.

In the second room, the large back wall is covered by a fresco in the form of a lunette, depicting the *Adoration of the Magi,* with a long procession above a niche used as a tabernacle. In the tabernacle there is a fresco of *Christ rising from the Sepulchre, with the symbols of the Passion.* At the foot of a craggy mountain, the procession of wise men unfolds in the horizontal rhythm so dear to Angelico. The variegated and varicoloured procession is composed of multi-ethnic wise men and their retinue, guided by three kings, prostrated and kneeling before the Infant Jesus, offering gifts. It is well known that the subject was quite dear to the Medici, and they willingly identified with the Magi bringing gifts to God. This subject, depicted in Cosimo's cell, could have easily been the symbol of the gift Cosimo offered to God: the support given to the Dominicans for the convent of San Marco, and consequently, a convenient way of glorifying him. The procession also provided witness

Interior of Cell 38;
on the left
is the entrance to Cell 39.

Crucifixion with the Virgin and Saints Cosmas, John, and Peter of Verona

to an extraordinary event that took place in Florence between 1439 and 1444: the Council for the unification with the Greek Church.

In the centre of the procession, where the vanishing lines converge, there is a mysterious astronomer with an armillary sphere, perhaps Zarathustra, who, using the stars, predicted the coming of a Saviour.

The stylistic reading of the fresco is not easy due to the damaged and non-finished areas, such as the Virgin's mantle, now devoid of the finale azurite layer. Many scholars maintain that the work is the result of collaboration between Angelico and Benozzo Gozzoli, with the help of an assistant. In my opinion, also considering of the number of *giornate* required to execute the fresco, there must have been various artists contributing to the work. Among these was certainly Angelico, whose participation does not seem to end with the compositional concept. The young king in profile standing in the foreground can be firmly attributed to him, both for the nobility in his stance as well as the refined and careful drawing. The young king's face shows a close affinity with the Magdalene's face in the fresco in Cell 1, *Noli me tangere*. There are similar technical and stylistic characteristics found in two central figures: the one with the braid seen from the back, and the figure of Saint Joseph. The other two kings and the Madonna and Child are much more abbreviated and can be attributed to one or two collaborators. The expressive features and gestures of all the figures on the right, even though painted with quick brushstrokes and reduced detail, I believe can be attributed to Gozzoli, the same artist responsible for the entire fresco of the *Crucifixion* in Cell 38.

Adoration of the Magi

Adoration of the Magi *(Cell 39)*,
detail of the three kings.

Adoration of the Magi *(Cell 39)*,
detail of the procession of the wise men.

Cell 40 – *Crucifixion with the Holy Women, Saint Dominic and the Centurions*

THIS IS THE FIRST OF FOUR CRUCIFIXIONS painted in the cells on this side of the corridor. The most dramatic moments of the event related in the Gospels of Luke and John are depicted as if evoked by the mind of Saint Dominic, who is portrayed in varying types of prayer among the historical onlookers.

This fresco and the ones that follow are larger in dimension, and the composition is spread out over a greater space. The scene is rendered surreal by the white background, with the symbolically darkened sun above the cross.

The attention is concentrated on the swooning Virgin who is held up by Mary Magdalene and Mary of Cleophas, and on the awe-struck centurions kneeling at the right. The emotional focus of the entire scene is on Saint Dominic, prostrated in front of the cross in a gesture that corresponds to the second method of praying laid out in *De modo orandi*, the desire for penitence for one's faults.

Even though the colour loss makes legibility more difficult, the fresco is painted in a broad, synthetic manner very close to the language of Angelico. Part of the execution was probably delegated to Benozzo Gozzoli, who certain scholars (Padoa Rizzo, Bonsanti) believe participated in the concept as well.

Crucifixion with the Holy Women, Saint Dominic and the Centurions, *detail of the Holy Women.*

Crucifixion with the Holy Women, Saint Dominic and the Centurions

Cell 41 – *Crucifixion with the Virgin, Mary Magdalene and Saint Dominic*

THIS FRESCO DEPICTS A PARTICULARLY emotional moment of the Crucifixion when Jesus pronounces the word 'thirst', painted by the artist on his chest.

One of the onlookers, not understanding the metaphorical meaning of the request – the thirst for God – responds by mockingly offering a sponge soaked in vinegar (Jn. 19, 28-30). On the left, Saint Dominic looks at the Crucifix with his arms folded over his chest in an attitude of great emotional participation. Even the Virgin and the Mary Magdalene are portrayed together in a sorrowful and prayerful attitude.

The fine lines and Christ's rounded face, direct us towards the work of a collaborator, who in this case, cannot be identified as Benozzo Gozzoli.

Crucifixion with the Virgin, Mary Magdalene and Saint Dominic, *detail of the sorrowful Virgin and Magdalene.*

Crucifixion with the Virgin, Mary Magdalene and Saint Dominic

Cell 42 – *Crucifixion with Mary, Martha and Saint Dominic*

ANOTHER MOMENT OF THE CRUCIFIXION is illustrated in this fresco (Jn. 19, 31-34), where the centurion thrusts the lance into Christ's side, and even though he is dead, the wound drips blood and water. The dramatic character of the scene stems more from the isolated positioning of the figures than from exasperated gestures. Angelico illuminates the figures with a surreal light, sculpting out the forms. The attention is centred on the centurion rather than the Crucifix, underlining the cruelty of the act, and in the fulfilment of the prophetic words 'They will look upon him whom they have pierced'. The splendid figures of Mary and Martha united by their mutual sorrow, are accentuated by the figure of Martha with her back turned. Not only does the figure of Saint Dominic, his hands joined in prayer before the Crucifix, invite us to meditation, but also the figure of an elderly, unidentified saint on the left, who gestures with his hand to the Crucifix. The high quality of this painting and the synthetic and rarefied style point to a work executed almost entirely by Angelico.

Crucifixion with Mary, Martha and Saint Dominic, *detail of the sorrowful Mary and Martha.*

Crucifixion with Mary, Martha and Saint Dominic

Crucifixion with Mary, the Magdalene, Saints John and Dominic

Cell 43 – *Crucifixion with Mary, the Magdalene, Saints John and Dominic*

THE ARTIST'S ATTENTION HERE IS CONCENTRATED on Mary's sorrow in the face of her son's sacrifice, and on the solidarity of Mary Magdalene and John. Once again the image seems to refer to Jesus' words to his mother: 'Woman, behold your son', and to his disciple: 'Son, this is your mother' (Jn. 19, 26-27). On the right Saint Dominic is kneeling completely absorbed in meditation.

The insecure drawing, evident in Mary's arms, together with the pictorial and expressive simplification exclude the possibility of Angelico's direct participation and point us towards an unidentified collaborator, whom I believe cannot be Benozzo Gozzoli.

Cell 44 – *Saint Dominic praying before the Crucifix*

This fragment of a fresco must have originally depicted *Saint Dominic praying before the Crucifix*, and compositionally is similar to the previous one.

Unfortunately, today only Saint Dominic remains, with his arms out-stretched towards a Crucifix that was lost in the demolition of the wall to make a new window, following the closure of the previous one when the stairs were constructed or modified at some indefinite point in time.

Saint Dominic praying before the Crucifix

East Corridor-Corridor of the Clerics
Wall painting of the *Madonna delle Ombre*

THE VISIT TO THE FRESCOES by Fra Angelico ends in the middle of the Corridor of the Clerics, with the *Sacred Conversation*, called the *Madonna delle Ombre*, positioned on the wall over brightly-coloured imitation marble mouldings. The work is probably the last one painted by Angelico and it is unusual in both technique and style. Compositionally, it is similar to altarpieces executed in tempera on wood panel. The reason why the artist chose to paint in tempera on a wall prepared 'a fresco', is still unknown. Perhaps he wished to imitate the chromatic results of an altarpiece, certainly more intense and less transparent than in fresco painting.

The Virgin and Child are seated on a marble throne in front of a niche with a gilt basin, reminiscent of the reflected light of a mosaic. The aedicula of the throne is decorated with an arabesque of scrolling foliage, also found on the decoration of the painted buildings in Angelico's Vatican frescoes. The throne is placed against a white wall, rhythmically divided by fluted pilasters and capitals with stylised leaves. Its shadow is realistically cast onto the wall, hence the title *Madonna delle Ombre* (*Madonna of the Shadows*). On the Virgin's lap, the delicately featured Infant Jesus is in the act of blessing. They are flanked on either side by two groups of saints, in peaceful conservation among themselves. On the far left, Saint Dominic, holding a lily, points to the words of his own spiritual testament, written in the book he holds in his hand. Next to him are Cosmas and Damian, the protectors of the Medici family, followed by Mark, the patron saint of the convent holding open his Gospel. Continuing on

the right, John the Evangelist with an open book, is followed by Thomas Aquinas, Doctor of the Order, by Lawrence, patron saint of Lorenzo de' Medici, benefactor of the convent with his brother Cosimo, and Peter of Verona, Dominican martyr, defender of orthodoxy.

The similarity to the altarpiece made for the main altar in the church is quite evident, however here, due to the shallowness of the viewing space in the corridor, the artist demonstrates even greater compositional ability. The light grazes across the figures, in the same position as the natural light from the large window at the end of the corridor. The volumes are sculpted in *chiaroscuro* effects that are both decisive and soft, obtained through the subtle modelling from the most vibrant light to shadow, creating metallic reflections on the haloes and the basin. The painting seems to be constructed by the movement of colour and light, reducing the very elegant drawing to a minimal, as seen in the rendering of the tapered hands. Unfortunately, the shadow effects on the vermilion red and violet mantles have been lost.

The fresco's unnerving modernity, the classical architecture and the effects of the light, are elements of the *maestro*'s style during the later 1440s. At times, these elements have led to a later dating, after the 1450s and Angelico's return from Rome. However, this is not the only feasible hypothesis, especially in light of its relation to the altarpiece in the church, completed in 1443, as well as the close rapport with the other frescoes in the cells. Thus, the motivations do not seem to be sufficient enough to retain that a fresco, so connected to the glorification of the Medici, would have been executed so many years after the conclusion of the work, which was, at the latest in 1444.

Madonna delle Ombre,
detail of the Infant Jesus blessing.

Christ on the Cross
adored by Saint Dominic,
detail of Christ's face;
Cloister of Sant'Antonino.

Bibliography

G. VASARI, *Le Vite de' più eccellenti pittori, scultori e architetti* (Florence 1568), edited by G. Milanesi, Florence 1878, vol. II, pp. 507-508.

F. BOCCHI, *Le bellezze della città di Firenze*, Florence 1591.

F. BALDINUCCI, *Notizie dei professori del disegno da Cimabue in qua* (Florence 1681), edited by F. Ranalli, Florence 1845-1847, pp. 414-423.

V. MARCHESE, *San Marco; Convento de' Padri predicatori in Firenze illustrato e inciso principalmente nei dipinti del B. Giovanni Angelico, con la vita dello stesso pittore e un sunto storico del Convento medesimo*, Florence 1851-1853.

J. A. CROWE-G. B. CAVALCASELLE, *Storia della pittura in Italia dal secolo II al secolo XVI*, Florence 1883, pp. 353-422.

S. BEISSEL, *Fra' Giovanni Angelico, sein Leben uns seine Werke*, Freiburg in Breisgau 1895.

R. LANGTON DOUGLAS, *Fra' Angelico*, London 1900.

F. SCHOTTMÜLLER, *Frau Angelico da Fiesole: Des Meisters Gemalde. Klassiker der Kunst in Gesamtausgabe*, Stuttgart 1911.

R. MORCAY, *La "Cronaca" del Convento fiorentino di San Marco: la parte più antica dettata da Giuliano Lapaccini*, in "Archivio Storico italiano", LXXI, 1913, pp. 1-29.

R. VAN MARLE, *The development of the Italian Schools of Painting*, 19 vols., The Hague 1923-1926, vol. X, p. 89.

P. MURATOFF, *Fra' Angelico*, London-New York 1930.

M. L. GENGARO, *Il Beato Angelico a San Marco*, Bergamo 1944.

A. M. FRANCINI CIARANFI, *Gli affreschi di San Marco a Firenze*, Milan 1947.

M. SALMI, *Problemi dell'Angelico*, in "Commentari", I, 1950, pp. 75-81 and 146-156.

J. POPE-HENNESSY, *Fra' Angelico*, London 1952; 2nd ed., London 1974.

G. C. ARGAN, *Fra' Angelico,* Geneva 1955.

U. BALDINI, in *Mostra delle opere di Fra' Angelico nel quinto centenario della morte,* exhibition catalogue (Rome, April- May 1955), Florence 1955, pp. 95-99.

G. URBANI, *Beato Angelico,* Milan 1957.

M. SALMI, *Il Beato Angelico,* Spoleto 1958.

B. BERENSON, *The Italian Pictures of the Renaissance. The Florentine School,* London 1963, p. 13.

S. ORLANDI, O. P., *Beato Angelico. Monografia storica della vita e delle opere, con un'appendice di nuovi documenti inediti,* Florence 1964.

L. BERTI-B. BELLARDONI-E. BATTISTI, *Angelico a San Marco,* Rome 1965.

L. BERTI, *Angelico,* Florence 1967.

A. PADOA RIZZO, *Una precisazione sulla collaborazione di Benozzo agli affreschi del Convento di San Marco,* in "Antichità viva", VII, 1969, pp. 9-13.

U. BALDINI, *L'opera completa dell'Angelico,* Milan 1970.

G. BONSANTI, *Firenze, l'Angelico al Convento di San Marco,* Novara 1982.

G. BONSANTI, *Preliminari per l'Angelico restaurato,* in "Arte cristiana", 71, 1983, pp. 25-34.

Beato Angelico: Miscellanea di studi, edited by Postulazione Generale dei Domenicani. Pontificia commissione centrale per l'arte sacra in Italia, Rome 1984, pp. 351-405.

L. BELLOSI, *Il Museo di San Marco,* in "Prospettiva", 37, 1984, pp. 87-88.

T. S. CENTI, O.P., *Il Beato Giovanni pittore Angelico (Biografia critica),* Siena 1984.

M. J. MAREK, *Ordenspolitik und andacht. Frau Angelicos Kreuzigungsfresko im Kapitelsaal von San Marco zu Florenz,* in "Zeitschrift fur Kunstgeschichte", 48, 1985, pp. 451-475.

D. DINI-G. BONSANTI, *Fra' Angelico e gli affreschi nel Convento di San Marco (ca. 1441-1450),* in *Tecnica e Stile. Esempi di pittura murale del Rinascimento italiano,* I, compiled by E. Borsook and F. Superbi Gioffredi, Florence 1986, pp. 17-24.

La chiesa e il convento di San Marco a Firenze, 2 vols., Florence 1989-1990.

L. CASTELFRANCHI VEGAS, *L'Angelico e l'Umanesimo,* Milan 1989.

G. BONSANTI, *Gli affreschi del Beato Angelico,* in *La chiesa e il convento di San Marco a Firenze,* vol. II, Florence 1990, pp. 115-172.

G. DIDI-HUBERMAN, *Fra' Angelico. Dissemblance et figuration,* Paris 1990.

D. DINI-M. SCUDIERI, *Gli affreschi di San Marco nella storia del restauro,* in *Le pitture murali. Tecniche, problemi, conservazione,* Florence 1990, pp. 269-288.

A. PADOA RIZZO, *Benozzo Gozzoli: catalogo completo,* Florence 1992.

W. HOOD, *Fra' Angelico at San Marco,* New Haven 1993.

M. BOSKOVITS, *Immagini da meditare,* Milan 1994.

P. MORACHIELLO, *Beato Angelico. Gli affreschi di San Marco,* Milan 1995.

Gli affreschi del Beato Angelico nel Convento di San Marco a Firenze, compiled by D. Dini, Turin 1996.

L. BELLOSI, *Una testimonianza su Dino Dini e sull'Angelico a San Marco,* in *Gli affreschi del Beato Angelico nel Convento di San Marco a Firenze,* compiled by D. Dini, Turin 1996, pp. 19-28.

J. T. SPIKE, *Angelico,* Milan 1996.

G. BONSANTI, *Beato Angelico,* Florence 1998.

C. B. STRELKE, *Angelico,* Milan 1998.

G. CORNINI, *Beato Angelico,* supplement to "Art e Dossier", no. 155, April 2000.

E. MARINO, O. P., *Il Beato Angelico. Saggio sul rapporto persona-opere visive ed opere visive-persona,* Pistoia 2001.

Benozzo Gozzoli allievo a Roma, maestro in Umbria, edited by B. Toscano and G. Capitelli, Milan 2002.

M. BOSKOVITS, *Il Beato Angelico e Benozzo Gozzoli: problemi ancora aperti* e *La bottega del Beato Angelico tra Firenze e Roma, e la formazione di Benozzo Gozzoli,* in *Benozzo Gozzoli allievo a Roma, maestro in Umbria,* Milan 2002, pp. 41-55 and 133-141.